Ezra Jack Keats

Dean Engel and Florence B. Freedman

Ezra Jack Keats

A Biography with Illustrations

Dean Engel and Florence B. Freedman

 Silver Moon Press

Mr. Keats's illustrations provided by the de Grummond Children's Literature Research Collection at the University of Southern Mississippi and the private collections of Dean Engel and Florence B. Freedman.

First Silver Moon Press edition 1995

Copyright © 1995 by ...   *Dean Engel and Florence B. Freedman*

For information write:

Silver Moon Press
126 Fifth Avenue, Suite 803
New York, NY 10011
(800) 874-3320

Design: Tsang/Seymour Design Studio, NYC

Printed in The Republic of Korea

10 9 8 7 6 5 4 3 2 1

Library of Congress Cataloging-in-Publication Data

Engel, Dean, 1943-
    Ezra Jack Keats : a biography with illustrations / Dean Engel and Florence B. Freedman. -- 1st Silver Moon Press ed.
        p.   cm.
        ISBN 1-881889-65-3
        1.Keats, Ezra Jack--Biography--Juvenile literature. 2. Authors, American--20th century--Biography--Juvenile literature.
3. Illustrators--United States--Biography--Juvenile literature.
4. Children's stories--Authorship--Juvenile literature.
5. Illustration of books--Juvenile literature.[1.Keats, Ezra Jack. 2. Authors, American. 3. Illustrators.] I. Freedman, Florence B. (Florence Bernstein) II. Title.
PS3561.E25243Z66   1994
741.6'42'092--dc20
[B]
                                                                                94-34960
                                                                                CIP
                                                                                    AC

To Ezra whose final request of me was to tell him a story, and to Florence without whom this story could not be told.   - D.E.

Table of Contents

Prologue

Ezra Jack Keats had blue eyes, warm, gentle hands and a long, grey moustache that curled up when he was happy and down when he was sad. He lived in an apartment high above the streets of Manhattan with his big orange cat, Samantha.

In his studio, filled with letters and drawings from children around the world, Ezra created books — books about children. He worked every day surrounded by sketches and brushes and tubes of paint, his beloved Samantha asleep at his side.

From humble beginnings in Brooklyn, New York, Ezra became a writer and illustrator of international acclaim. When he died in 1983, he had created over twenty books and illustrated many more. The first book he both wrote and

illustrated, *The Snowy Day*, won the Caldecott Medal, the highest honor in children's literature.

The authors of this book knew Ezra as a student, colleague, and friend. The story that follows is based on conversations with him and on autobiographical essays.

ABOVE: Ezra and Samantha in their Manhattan studio.

Chapter One

A Bottle of Ink

Ezra Jack Keats was born Jack Ezra Katz in Brooklyn, New York on March 11, 1916. He was the youngest of three children born to immigrant Polish Jews. His father, Benjamin, waited tables in a coffee shop on the Lower East Side of Manhattan. He worked long hours and earned very little money.

Some of Ezra's earliest memories were of his family gathered around the coal stove in the kitchen of their modest Brooklyn apartment. The coal stove was the center of activity in winter because it was the only source of heat. Benjamin sat reading his newspaper, *The Jewish Daily Forward*, while Ezra's mother Augusta — or Gussie, as she was called — ironed on an old wooden board. Ezra's brother, Willie, and sister, Mae, did their homework at the kitchen table. And Ezra did what he liked best — he drew pictures.

Pictures began to appear — a bird, a steamship, an airplane.
(Detail of endpapers, *Goggles!*, 1969.)

During the winter, he slept on a cot near the coal stove because he was frail and caught cold easily.

One night, Ezra awoke and found he was alone. He listened for a moment but heard nothing. *Where is everybody?* he wondered. Then he remembered. Willie was staying overnight at a friend's and everyone else was visiting neighbors across the hall.

The kitchen was dark except for the light from a streetlight outside. It shone onto the enamel-topped table where a small bottle of ink glistened and glowed and beckoned to Ezra. Next to the bottle lay a pen. He'd have to act quickly. Gussie would be in any minute to check on him.

He scrambled to the table, grabbed the pen and dipped it in the ink. It seemed to glide across the table. Pictures began to appear — a bird, a steamship, an airplane.

Ezra drew frantically until the table was covered in ink. When he stopped, he realized what he'd done. His mother's clean white table! He'd really catch it now.

He climbed back onto his cot, pulled the covers up to his ears, pretended to be asleep and listened anxiously for his parents' return.

Soon he heard footsteps. "Look what the boy did to your table," his father shouted. "Make him wash it off first thing in the morning. He can't get away with such mischief."

"He'll catch it from Willie in the morning for using up all his ink!" Mae said.

But Gussie said in a soft voice, "I think it's beautiful."

Ezra's parents often argued after the kids went to bed. Most nights Ezra only listened drowsily, but tonight he caught every word. Tonight, they argued about him.

"Don't say such things. You'll only encourage him," Benjamin cried. "What good will his pictures do him? Will they put food in his mouth when he is grown? Better he should learn a trade, like Willie."

Benjamin thought Willie was a sensible boy with a good head for figures. He'd be able to get a job and take care of himself. But Benjamin worried about Ezra and Mae.

At that time, most girls married and had husbands to take care of them. But what would happen if Mae did not marry? How would she support herself?

And Ezra had these silly notions about painting. He'd never earn a living painting pictures. Painting signs maybe, but pictures? Never!

The argument continued into the night.

"Go ahead, Gussie. Make a bum out of the boy if you want."

"Shh... Papa, he'll hear you."

"Let him hear me! Maybe he'll get some sense in his head."

The next morning Ezra stayed in bed under the covers until his father left for work.

"Get up, Ezra! You'll be late for school," Gussie urged. Ezra washed and dressed. He was very surprised when he heard his mother say, "I think your pictures are beautiful and I'm going to preserve them. I'll cover them with the Sabbath tablecloth and show them to everybody who comes to the house. But we won't say any more about it to Papa. You might be a real artist someday, and you'll remember this as your first exhibition."

Ezra asked, "You're not mad that I dirtied the table?"

"No. But Papa is mad. He doesn't want you to be an artist. I can't blame him. He sees lots of artists everyday at the coffee shop. Most of them are hungry and out of work. They have coffee for breakfast and soup for dinner. Papa doesn't want that life for you. I can see that you like to draw, and so you must continue. But, it will be our little secret from now on."

"What about Willie's ink?" Ezra said.

"I'll make it up to him," Gussie said reassuringly. "Now go to school and be a good boy."

Despite Benjamin's objections, Gussie encouraged Ezra to draw and paint each day after school. And every night before Ben came home from work, Gussie and Ezra hid the paints under the stairs in the hall. Then they opened the windows wide and chased the telltale odor of turpentine out into the night air.

Before long, a neighbor uncovered their secret. She found Ezra's paints under the stairs. Gussie was relieved and proudly invited her in to see Ezra's work. Word of the young artist who lived upstairs spread fast.

Encouraged by this sudden fame, Ezra now drew everywhere — on newspapers, shoe boxes, brown paper bags, and pieces of burlap that local shopkeepers saved for him. He spent all his free time copying other artists' drawings that he found in magazines. It was what he liked to do best.

Chapter Two

Running Away

It seemed to Ezra that nobody at home paid much attention to him unless he drew something. And then, his mother would praise him, and Benjamin would scold him.

"Why don't you go out and play ball like other kids?" he'd bellow.

Most times Ezra felt invisible — like invisible ink you bought in the candy store — the kind spies used to write secret messages. You had to breathe on it to see it.

In school one day Ezra read a story about a little boy who ran away from home. It seemed like a good idea to him. Besides, nobody would care. They probably wouldn't even notice he was gone. He saw himself, like the boy in the story, striding down the road with a pole balanced on his shoulder. Tied to the pole — a bundle containing his prized possessions.

Ezra began to plan his trip. What would he take? His wooden matchsticks, of course. Every time Benjamin lit a cigarette, or Gussie lit the coal stove, Ezra confiscated the extinguished matches. He glued them together and made log cabins, forts, and tracks for his imaginary trains.

He'd also take a deck of cards. If he met somebody along the way, they could play a game or two, and when he was alone, he could make up stories about the King of Spades and the knights. And, of course, he would take his paints.

What would he do for a pole and cloth to tie his things in? He'd borrow one of Gussie's kitchen towels and the old mop she didn't use anymore. The mop handle would do just fine.

Ezra planned his trip for days. Finally, he was ready. He wrapped his things in the kitchen towel, tied the towel to the mop, and hid it under his cot. He would leave the next morning.

But he would have to say goodbye to Gussie. What would she say? Would she cry and beg him not to go? Would she say, "You're my little boy and I love you? Please don't run away." Would he change his mind if she did?

The next morning, Gussie was on her knees scrubbing the floor when Ezra approached her. "Ma," he said, "I'm running away."

Gussie looked him over carefully. "That bundle is going to fall apart. Here, let me tie it tighter." She tightened the knot and then went right back to her scrubbing. Did she think he was kidding? She didn't seem to mind that he was

running away! Well, he didn't mind either. Someday, he'd
return rich and famous in a big automobile. Then she'd appre-
ciate him. Ezra squared his shoulders and walked downstairs
into the street.

Outside he saw some neighborhood bullies walking toward
him. These guys were tough and everybody knew it. How he
wished his big brother Willie was there to scare them off!

ABOVE: One of the bullies knocked Ezra down and grabbed his bundle.
(Detail from *Goggles!*, 1969.)

Willie was Ezra's protector in those days. His nickname was Kelly after a red-haired comic strip character popular at the time. If a kid was bullying Ezra and someone yelled, "Here comes Kelly!" the kid ran for his life. Kelly knew how to give fierce wrist burns. He'd wrap his hands around a kid's wrist and twist in opposite directions. Nobody wanted to risk getting one of Kelly's wrist burns.

One of the bullies knocked Ezra down and grabbed his bundle. His matchsticks and paints went flying!

"Cards!" shouted one of the toughs. "Let's have a game. Don't worry, kid. We'll give 'em back after we're done."

Ezra carefully fished his matchsticks and paints out of the gutter. He waited silently. Finally, one of the bullies got bored and left. "Here's your chance, kid," another said. "Now you can play with us." It sounded more like a threat than an invitation. "Okay," Ezra said, "but I can't stay long."

They played on. Ezra was getting hungry and the sky was getting dark. Finally, the bullies abandoned the game. Ezra put his cards back into his bundle, tied it really tight this time, and started off again.

He turned off Vermont Street and walked a few blocks. Suddenly, he realized he was on Wyona Street — enemy territory! Every block had its own gang. They'd pounce on a kid from foreign turf and make him sorry he strayed. A black eye or bloody nose was the usual punishment for trespassing.

"Hey, guys, look — Vermonter!" someone shouted and the Wyona Street gang began chasing Ezra.

Suddenly, he realized he was on Wyona Street — enemy territory!
(Spread from *The Trip*, 1978.)

He ran as fast as he could, tripped, almost fell, steadied himself, and with a desperate burst of speed left the Wyona Street gang behind in a cloud of dust.

He sighed with relief when he found himself back on Vermont Street. It was dark now. He saw the light in his kitchen window. He hated to go home, but what else could he do? Maybe he would run away tomorrow.

He climbed the stairs slowly and tried to open the door. It was locked. He knocked.

"Who is it?" Gussie asked.

"It's me, Ezra." There was silence.

"It's me, Ezra, your son."

"You can't be Ezra. Ezra ran away."

He heard the bolt on the door clack shut.

"Ma, open up. Please."

He could see Gussie's shadow through the glass panel in the door. She just stood there. He rattled the doorknob as hard as he could. Then he banged on the door with his fists until they hurt, shouting desperately, "Please give me another chance. I'll never run away again."

Finally, Ezra heard his father say, "Let him in." The door opened.

"Wash up and get to bed!" Benjamin ordered, not even looking up from his newspaper.

Nothing had changed. Ezra was still invisible, but at least now he was safe.

Chapter Three

Tzadik

The next morning Ezra unpacked his bundle. It was Saturday, and there was no school. From the kitchen window he saw kids across the street jumping up and down on cellar doors — metal plates hinged into the sidewalk that covered steps leading underground to the cellar. He decided to go see about all the commotion.

Kids were taking turns springing up and down on the cellar doors, marking the height of their jumps on the wall with chalk. They invited Ezra to jump, too. But as he got ready to jump, the cellar doors sprang open, and he was hurled onto the sidewalk. Everyone scattered.

A huge, bearded man with flowing red hair erupted from the blackness below, shouting, "Wild animals! Can't a man pray in peace?"

It was Tzadik — the Religious One. The Strange One.

A huge, bearded man with flowing red hair erupted from the blackness below. (Spread from *Louie's Search*, 1980.)

Tzadik lived in the cellar where he stored the coal and wood he sold to the neighborhood for fuel. People often heard him singing Hebrew prayers in a rich, powerful voice while he worked.

Ezra was trembling. He picked himself up, ran a few steps, tripped and fell. Tzadik straddled him, pinning him to

16

ABOVE: His gaze ended at Tzadik's long, red beard, broad face, and masses of curly red hair. (Detail from *Louie's Search*, 1980.)

the ground between his enormous feet. Ezra looked up from Tzadik's knobby toes, bristling with red hairs and jutting from broken shoes, to his tremendous legs covered by baggy pants, tied with clothesline. His gaze ended at Tzadik's long, red beard, broad face, and masses of curly red hair.

Tzadik spoke softly, his words coming down to Ezra from far away. "God put us on this earth to help each other, not hurt each other." Then, without warning, he swooped down and lifted Ezra high into the air. "Look up! See! God is there." Ezra looked up at the sky. A small white cloud floated by. "He didn't put us on this earth to be good-for-nothings," Tzadik continued. "Remember! Serve the Lord." Ezra looked down at Tzadik. The huge man's intense blue eyes seemed to bore right through him.

"Repeat after me: 'Worship the Lord. The Lord is merciful'."

Ezra, dangling from Tzadik's huge hands, sputtered, "Worship the Lord. The Lord is merciful."

Tzadik gently set Ezra down on the ground and sighed, "God watch over you, little herring." Ezra was relieved, but he didn't run away. Instead, he watched as Tzadik strode over to a pile of discarded furniture, picked up an armload of wood, and disappeared into the cellar singing.

Ezra followed Tzadik's oversized footsteps and walked over to what was left of the pile. He found a small wooden panel — maybe part of a door — and tucked it under his arm as he hurried home singing.

Gussie was washing clothes when he got there. Ezra didn't mention Tzadik. Instead, he got out his paint box, grabbed a few brushes, a piece of cardboard for a palette, and his panel of wood, and climbed out the window onto the fire escape.

He could hear Tzadik's words as he looked up at the sky beyond the flapping clotheslines, beyond the rooftops. *He didn't put us on this earth to be good-for-nothings. Remember! Serve the Lord.*

A small white cloud floated by. Ezra mixed some white and blue paint and covered the panel of wood with sky. He dipped his small brush in white and gently painted a cloud. Then he sat back.

He had created his first original painting.

He looked up and saw Gussie watching him.

"I was going to come out to hang the wash, but I didn't want to disturb you while you were painting. Why are you out here? Where did you get that wood?"

"I saw Tzadik pick up some broken furniture. He left this piece of wood behind."

"You didn't make fun of Tzadik, did you?"

"No, we had a good talk," Ezra replied.

"Oh. And what did you talk about?" Gussie asked.

"You know Tzadik. We talked about God. He said that God is watching us all the time."

They stood silently looking down at his painting, and up at the sky. Then Ezra helped Gussie hang out the wash.

Chapter Four

Neighborhood Friends

After his talk with Tzadik, Ezra spent more time creating original paintings. He painted what he saw — the tenements across the street with garbage cans out front and stoops filled with people. Painting was better than playing with other kids anyway. He wasn't good at sports and he was always left out when teams were chosen.

Ezra was about ten years old when he met his first best friend. New people moved into the apartment upstairs — Mr. Love, his wife, and their son, Teddy. A few weeks after they moved in, Mr. Love left and never came back.

Gussie felt sorry for Mrs. Love and wanted to help her. "Poor woman," she would say, "so pretty and nice. She doesn't know a soul in the neighborhood."

Mrs. Love found a job as a cashier in a restaurant, so

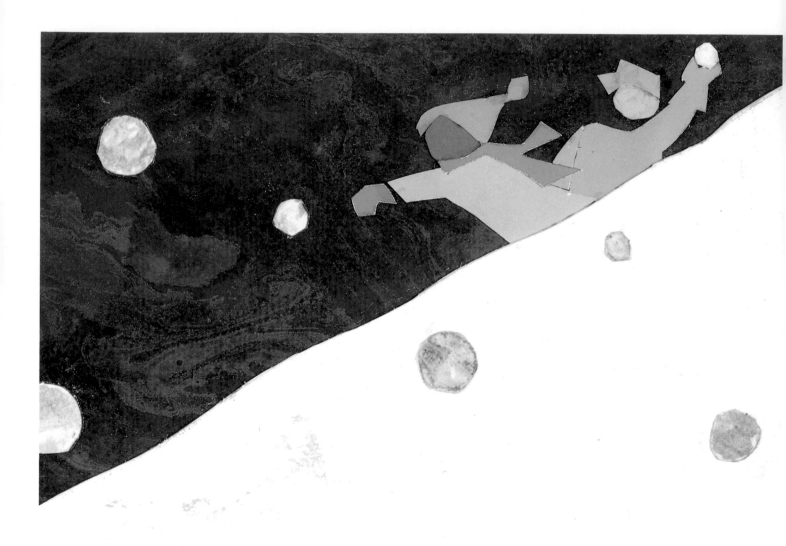

Ezra made round, hard snowballs and Teddy threw them with all his might, rarely missing his target. (Detail from *The Snowy Day*, 1962.)

Teddy stayed at Ezra's house every day after school. He told everybody he was Ezra's cousin.

One day he invited Ezra upstairs. The apartment was almost bare. The only furniture in the room where Teddy slept was a wooden chair, a small table with schoolbooks on it, and a folding cot. But the walls! Every inch of them was covered with magazine pictures of big, fancy automobiles. Teddy knew their names by heart.

"Which one do you like best?" Ezra asked.

"I like different parts of different ones," Teddy replied. "The car I really like..."

"Wait a minute," Ezra interrupted. "I'll get a pencil and paper." Following his instructions, Ezra sketched Teddy's dream car, taking fenders from one, the hood from another, and the body from a third.

"Wow! It's perfect," cried Teddy as he made a place for it on the wall.

Ezra and Teddy became best friends. In winter they played in the snow. They built snow forts which they defended against attackers. Ezra made round, hard snowballs and Teddy threw them with all his might, rarely missing his target.

On Saturdays they got ten cents each for the movies. The Supreme on Livonia Avenue showed double features, the *News of the Week*, *Coming Attractions*, and a cowboy serial that always ended at the most exciting part – a real cliffhanger! Sometimes Ezra and Teddy hid from the usher and saw the whole show twice.

The rest of the week Ezra entertained the kids on the block by re-telling the movie plots. Maybe he couldn't fight, and maybe he wasn't good at sports — but he sure could tell stories! Ezra was becoming more popular with everyone except the bullies, of course. They weren't interested in him or his stories. They were interested in Teddy who was bigger and stronger. They wanted him to join their gang and beat up the kids around the block.

One hot summer night they came for Teddy. Ezra was sitting with him on their stoop. The streetlight was broken. It was almost pitch black. A bunch of guys approached them. Lefty, the gang leader, brushed Ezra aside like a fly.

"You gonna hang around with this little sissy?" Lefty challenged Teddy, poking him in the stomach with a club. Teddy croaked, "Yeah, what's it to you?" Arms and clubs went flying. Ezra heard the gang beating Teddy with their bats. Still, he managed to get in a few punches as he tried to block the blows. He fought like crazy. Finally, the gang retreated.

Ezra and Teddy just stood there for a few minutes saying nothing. Then, Ezra said, "I'm sorry, Teddy. I should have tried to help you, but I couldn't move. It was like I was frozen."

"That's okay," Teddy answered. "You don't have to be a fighter. You've got other things to do. You do the drawing and the storytelling, and I'll do the fighting."

After that, Ezra and Teddy were inseparable until the

day Mrs. Love came to say they were moving. She thanked Gussie for being such a good friend but didn't say where they were going.

"I hope that no-good husband of hers sent for them," Gussie sighed.

"Wherever I am, I'll always hang your picture of my dream car in the middle of my wall," Teddy said to Ezra, "and we'll be friends forever." But they never saw each other again.

What would the bullies do to Ezra now that Teddy was gone? He soon found out.

One day as he was walking with a package under his arm, a couple of tough guys moved in on him. "Hey, watcha got there?" they asked.

Ezra unwrapped the package. It was one of his paintings. The guys looked at it, then at Ezra, then at each other. "Hey, d'you do that? Ain't that somethin'!"

None of the bullies bothered Ezra anymore. His paintings were his passport through the neighborhood.

Ezra soon made a new friend. He heard harmonica music coming from an apartment on the ground floor in his building.

One day when he was in the hallway listening, an apartment door swung opened and a tall, thin man appeared. Ezra had never seen him before.

"Who's there?" the man asked. "Who's outside my door?"

"My name's Ezra. I live upstairs. I was listening to you play."

"Well, don't just stand there like a stranger. Come in and sit down. I'll play a while, and then we can have some tea."

Ezra sat in a big, stuffed chair and listened. The man played on, staring right through Ezra as if he wasn't there. Slowly, Ezra realized that the man really *couldn't* see him. He was blind.

"Now we'll have some tea," said the man.

"Can I help you?" Ezra asked.

"No, thanks. I know my way around here," he answered. He walked to the cupboard and removed two cups and a box of cookies. Then he filled the kettle and placed it on the stove to boil. They sipped their tea in silence, but afterwards Ezra felt like they'd had a long talk.

"Well, I guess I'll be on my way now. I've gotta go to the grocery store for Ma," Ezra said.

"Someday if you want to go for a walk, knock on my door and I'll go with you. Okay?" the man asked.

The very next day Ezra and his new-found friend went for a walk. He was surprised by what the blind man could "see." Somehow he knew that the trees were budding.

"How can you tell?" asked Ezra.

"The wind sounds different in spring. The buds keep it from rushing through the trees. That's how I can tell — by the way the wind sounds. Besides, I can smell the fresh green budding leaves."

Ezra and his new friend took many walks together that spring.

Slowly, Ezra realized that the man really couldn't see him. He was blind. (Detail from *Apt. 3*, 1971.)

Chapter Five

The Depression

America's economic depression began in 1929, with the stock market crash. There was no work and no money. These were desperate days when people tucked old newspapers inside tattered overcoats to keep out the cold, and stuffed cardboard inside worn-out shoes to protect their feet from the rain.

Ezra was thirteen years old when the coffee shop where his father worked was forced to close.

Benjamin used to give Gussie his pay envelope every week. From that modest sum, she paid the rent, bought groceries, and hid what was left in a coffee tin under the kitchen sink. Now there were no pay envelopes.

One evening when the family gathered at the kitchen table for supper, Gussie burst into tears, crying, "There'll be

There was no work and no money. (Detail from *Louie's Search*, 1980.)

no supper tonight. We have nothing left." Ezra had never seen his mother cry before. It frightened him.

Benjamin rose slowly to his feet, lowered his head, and quietly left the table. Ezra sensed his father's shame and wanted to help. Willie worked part-time as a Western Union telegram messenger, but he was planning to marry soon. It was Ezra's turn to help. But he was a scrawny thirteen-year-old kid. Who would hire him?

The next morning, he dressed and hurried downstairs. Down the street came Mr. Goldman, with his horse drawn wagon piled high with luscious ripe watermelons, the first of the season. What a welcome sight they were in the grey, steamy streets of Brooklyn — cool, smooth, green melons cut into juicy, red slices!

"Ten cents a slice," shouted Mr. Goldman.

Ezra approached him shyly, "Morning, Mr. Goldman. Need any help? I'm looking for work."

"You and everybody else! Here, CATCH!" he shouted as he tossed one of his biggest watermelons into Ezra's arms.

Ezra staggered under the weight, but steadied himself quickly.

"Okay," said Mr. Goldman, "You're hired. A dollar a day and all the watermelons you can eat!"

That summer Ezra worked ten hours a day, six days a week. He had to load the wagon in the morning then unload it at night. The melons were kept in a cool cellar where Ezra soon discovered, huge, hungry rats ready to fight him for the booty. He was terrified of the rats but learned to scare them off.

Ezra gave Gussie the dollar he earned each day. It seemed as though the family treated him differently now. When he spoke at the supper table Willie didn't say, "Aw, pipe down. What do you know?" the way he used to. He was a wage earner now.

The days were long and the work was hard. Ezra grew pale and tired easily. Yet, in the quiet little kitchen, after everyone else had gone to bed, Ezra continued to paint.

He also continued his daily chores, one of which was to pick up milk from Mr. Abramowitz, the grocer. He didn't like going to Abramowitz's. Everyday, the grocer gave him a hard time because his family was running up a large bill. Even with Ezra and Willie helping, they were still just getting by.

"I know, I know," Abramowitz cried before Ezra could say a word. "Your father's out of work. You've got nothing to eat at home. Look, I'm a poor man, too. How is my family supposed to eat if folks like you don't pay their –"

Abramowitz stopped in mid-sentence.

"Hey, what have you got there? Where'd you get that?" he asked, pointing to the painting Ezra carried with him that day.

"I painted it."

"No kidding! You did that? Listen, you bring me a painting like that, and I'll take something off your bill. What d'ya say?"

During those difficult days, Ezra traded his paintings whenever possible and Benjamin stopped complaining about his son's passion for painting. He realized Ezra would continue to paint despite his protests. He also realized that Ezra's paintings had value — they could be traded for food.

"Well, if he's gotta paint," Benjamin said to Gussie, "he should know how to paint good." So one Sunday morning Benjamin and Ezra took the El (short for elevated train) to Manhattan. They went to the Metropolitan Museum of Art, which, according to Benjamin, had a lot of good paintings.

They explored the galleries for hours, studying portraits of famous men like George Washington, Thomas Jefferson, and Napoleon. Benjamin thought that paintings of great men were great paintings, and he urged Ezra to pay close attention to every detail. But Ezra grew bored with the paintings of these strange men in powdered wigs and velvet knickers, and he wandered on.

At the end of a long corridor marked *Nineteenth Century Painting*, he saw something he would never forget, a painting that seemed to glow. It was Honoré Daumier's *Third Class Carriage*.

He stood before the painting for a long time, staring at the three passengers in the wooden railway car. The painting told a story, he thought, and he tried to find the words. Finally, as if waking from a deep sleep, he heard his father's voice urging him to move on.

They turned a corner and found themselves in a gallery filled with 19th-century Impressionist paintings. The walls were covered with canvases by Renoir, Bonnard, and Monet.

It was Honoré Daumier's *Third Class Carriage*. (Ezra did this painting calling it *Copy of Daumier*. Oil on canvas.)

The paintings filled the gallery with color and light. Ezra's eyes grew wide with excitement. He had never heard of these artists, but their paintings, composed of daubs and strokes of color, drew him in. He could almost taste the thick, brilliant layers of paint. Someday he'd paint like that.

It was getting late. It was time for them to return home to the Brooklyn tenement with the naked light bulb in the hallway and the worn-down steps out front. It was time to go home.

Chapter Six

Discoveries

Ezra entered Junior High School 149 in the fall of 1929. Two important things happened to him there. He discovered the local branch of the Brooklyn Public Library, and he made a lifelong friend.

He had a crush on Harriet Towarski, a girl in his class. Harriet, who lived ten blocks from school, didn't even know he existed. He was too shy to approach her. She was very popular in school — always surrounded by friends. Instead, he strolled past her house every afternoon for weeks, hoping to catch a glimpse of her. When he finally did, he got so nervous he was speechless.

He never found the courage to approach Harriet. But on one of his afternoon strolls through her neighborhood, he made a wonderful discovery. He noticed a large imposing building too beautiful to be a school, too plain to be a church. Its wide steps led to huge wooden doors. He decided to investigate. As he approached, he saw these words on a plaque above the door: BROOKLYN PUBLIC LIBRARY, ARLINGTON BRANCH.

There wasn't a sound inside. A sign on the wall read *Reference Room* with an arrow pointing to the second floor.

He found the section marked *Art*, selected a few books, and sat down at a table to read. The books were about Ancient Art. He turned the pages, looking at the pictures and reading their captions: Egyptian, Greek, Roman....

Hours passed and the room grew dark. It was closing time. Ezra reluctantly closed his books — there was so much to learn! From then on, his afternoon strolls past Harriet's house often ended at the library.

In the summer of his first year in junior high, Ezra made a second wonderful discovery. He met a boy named Itz in summer school. Itz would become his lifelong friend.

Summer school was a place where students who failed a subject were given a chance to make it up. Ezra did well in most subjects, but math was a disaster. He didn't understand algebra, gave up trying, and failed the class.

There was a boy in class that summer who knew the subject very well, even before the teacher explained it. His name was Martin, but Ezra eventually nicknamed him "Itz." Itz wanted to be a scientist and was very good at math.

"Why are you here?" Ezra asked him. "You're good at algebra already."

They talked about many things, these new friends, the scientist and the artist. (Pen and ink sketch.)

"I know math all right," Itz replied. "I just don't know how to keep my mouth shut. I talked back to the teacher and he flunked me!"

"What happened?" Ezra asked.

"I was bored, so I started doing my science homework behind my algebra book," Itz said. The teacher caught me and bawled me out. I tried to explain that I knew the math and the class was boring."

Ezra and Itz became fast friends. They talked for hours after school. Itz walked Ezra home every afternoon. Then, having lots more to discuss, Ezra walked Itz home. And so on, back and forth, past supper. Ezra, the artist, pointed out the shades of blue in the sky, while Itz, the scientist, explained why it was blue.

In September, when school began, Ezra reveled in the colors of the autumn leaves. He knew the name of every color.

"Just look at those colors," Ezra said to his friend. And Itz proceeded to explain that all those colors were in the green leaves, and that when the chlorophyll was bleached out, the colors came through. He also explained how, before it dies, a leaf stands upright on its branch for just a moment and then, with no air to support it, flutters to the ground.

They talked about many things, these new friends, the artist and the scientist — about school, teachers, family — but mostly about girls.

Chapter Seven

Newspaper Clippings

At Thomas Jefferson High School, Ezra widened his circle of friends with students who, like himself, were interested in art, literature, and music. Above all, these young minds wanted to solve the world's social and political problems. They had long discussions in class about the events of the day — unemployment in the U.S. and the political and economic theories of democracy, socialism, and communism.

Ezra recorded the Great Depression in his paintings: an elderly man peddling sweet potatoes roasting on a bucket of hot coals; idle men, their workworn hands empty and lifeless.

He also painted a portrait of his parents during this period. His mother was willing. At first Benjamin resisted, then, finally agreed.

"Wait. I'll put on a shirt and tie to look more respectable, no?" he asked.

"No," said Ezra. "I want you just as you are."

"Wouldn't it be better if I wore a nice dress?" Gussie asked.

"Not at all," said Ezra. "I don't want a posed picture like you see in a photographer's window. I want to paint you the way I know you best — as you are right now."

They gave in and posed for his sketch — Benjamin in his undershirt, his suspenders hanging from his pants, and Gussie in a housedress and apron. Ezra hid the painting from them until it was finished. When he finally showed it to them, they seemed puzzled. Benjamin said, "Well, we certainly look natural." And Gussie added, "Anyone would know the artist was one of the family."

They invited neighbors and friends to see it. Mr. and Mrs. Max, whom they had known in Poland, came by for a cup of tea. This was a terrible mistake.

Sam Max was a jealous, bitter man who liked to drink. When he wasn't drinking, he was finding fault with everything and everybody. Mrs. Max was the wage earner. She plucked chickens at the butcher shop. They had no children.

"Well, what do you think of my son's painting?" Gussie asked proudly.

"Very nice," said Mrs. Max distractedly.

Mr. Max took advantage of being asked to give an

They gave in and posed for his sketch—Benjamin in his undershirt, his suspenders hanging from his pants, and Gussie in a house dress and apron.(Oil on canvas.)

opinion. He spent a long time looking at the painting, as though he were a real expert. He made no comment on Ezra's skillful technique or on the incredible likeness of the painting to its subjects. Instead, he said, "What? You don't own a shirt, Ben? And Gussie, you don't have a nicer dress? You look like a couple of bums dressed like that. I think your precious son is making fools of you!"

Mrs. Max rose nervously from her chair. "Now, Sam, calm down! It's a picture of plain, ordinary people at home. They're supposed to look like that." She took her husband's arm and started for the door. "We really have to go. We left Mazik home alone." Mazik was their cat.

After this outburst, the portrait was buried at the back of the closet and never shown again. Ezra wondered about the incident for a long time. He'd only wanted to please his parents, but somehow he'd hurt them instead.

It was no wonder he loved to escape to school, where his paintings were understood and appreciated. His art teacher sent photographs of his work to a famous New York artist named Max Weber. Ezra was surprised when he received an invitation from Weber to visit him at his Long Island home. Weber offered to meet him at the train station and urged him to bring along some of his paintings.

They spent the afternoon in the painter's studio. Ezra asked questions which a less patient artist might have ignored. Weber answered every one. He examined Ezra's paintings carefully and praised them. They talked about

Weber's years in Paris and about the famous artists he'd met there. Ezra hoped to visit Paris himself one day.

After lunch, Weber left Ezra at the train station with this advice: "You must keep on painting! Don't let anything discourage you."

Ezra never saw him again but went to all of his exhibitions. He never forgot the encouragement and kindness of this fine man.

He continued to work hard in school where his paintings were often on display. He was asked to paint a mural for the school auditorium. It remained there for many years.

In 1934, Ezra was chosen to represent Thomas Jefferson High School in the National Scholastic Art Competition. Schools across the country submitted drawings and paintings by their most talented students. Ezra's painting, *Shantytown*, depicted men huddled around a fire for warmth. It won first prize.

The school newspaper, *The Liberty Bell*, *The Brooklyn Eagle*, and *The Yiddish Press* ran articles about the competition. He thought Benjamin would surely see it in the *Jewish Daily Forward* which he read faithfully.

But nothing was ever said at home. Hadn't they seen it? Didn't it matter? Oh well — maybe they would notice when he won the Art Award next year at graduation.

But Ezra never got to graduation. Just two days before the ceremony, there was a knock at the door. A man's voice said: "Hello, Mrs. Katz. Is your son home? I have some

Shantytown won first prize in the National Scholastic Art Competition.
(Oil on canvas.)

burlap for him. He'd better come get it quick before somebody else does."

It was Abramowitz, the grocer. Ezra stepped out into the hallway as Abramowitz confessed, "I'm not here about burlap. It's about your father. He's at the shoemaker's and he's real sick. I don't want to scare your Ma."

Ezra had a terrible feeling in his stomach. "Is he dead?" he asked.

"Yes," Abramowitz said. "Your Pa's dead."

There was a crowd outside the shoemaker's when they arrived. Ezra saw his father's lifeless body inside, draped with his old, worn overcoat. The shoemaker put his hand on Ezra's shoulder. "Sorry, son," he said. "We had to get somebody from the family to identify the body. He must have had a heart attack or something. He stumbled in here and passed out."

Ezra couldn't say a word and coughed to hide a sob.

A policeman approached him and asked, "Do you know this man?"

"Yes, I know him. He's my father," Ezra answered in a choked voice.

"You'll have to check his wallet," said the policeman, handing it to Ezra.

He examined its contents. Two single dollar bills and newspaper clippings — lots of newspaper clippings about Ezra and the prizes he'd won.

Ezra looked long and hard at his father's body. He

stayed until the ambulance came. Then he walked home slowly, the events of the last hour playing over and over in his head like a movie.

Do you know this man? the policeman asked.

Ezra fingered the clippings from his father's wallet. This man who never openly approved of his painting carried news of his accomplishments with him each day. This man who never offered him a word of encouragement or praise saved every notice of his success.

Yes. I know him, Ezra answered the policeman's query. In reality, it seemed he and his father had only just met.

Chapter Eight

The Inker

It was 1935. Ezra had a high school diploma, the National Scholastic Art Competition Award, and a letter offering him a scholarship to the Art Students League in Manhattan.

He showed Gussie the letter. "I wish you could go," she said. "But it's impossible. There's no money coming in. Mae's still in school and Willie's married with family of his own to worry about."

Ezra took a deep breath and slumped over the table, his head in his hands.

"You have to get a job, Ezra," Gussie said. "Our rent is cheap, and we don't spend much on food. But we need you." "It'll be okay, Ma," Ezra said. He went out to walk and think. He knew he would never have this opportunity again, but he had to decline the scholarship.

He found work through a federal government agency —

the PWA, Public Works Administration. He helped paint murals on public buildings until 1939 when PWA projects were discontinued.

Not long after that, Ezra learned that a former classmate worked for a company called Five-Star Comics, the creators of the Captain Marvel comic book series. Ezra was interested in illustration and wanted to learn more about it.

"It's not much of a job," his friend told him, "but maybe they can use another man. I'll take you with me tomorrow. You'll have to bring some samples of your work — not those oil paintings and sketches though. You'd better do a few drawings suitable for comic strips. I'll show you how."

That night, with his friend's help, Ezra created a comic strip hero with bulging muscles and a sneaky villain with a long black moustache.

The next morning they arrived early at Five-Star Comics. They entered a dim loft filled with rickety drawing tables. About a dozen men wearing green eyeshades were hunched over the tables, working away.

Their boss, Mr. Chesler, liked Ezra's work. "Eighteen-fifty a week," he said. "Take it or leave it."

Ezra accepted the offer before Mr. Chesler could change his mind.

"You'll start as an inker," said the boss.

One of the men showed Ezra what an inker does. He is given a pencil sketch, drawn by the strip's creator. The sketch has been cleaned up by the "clean-up" man who erases any unnecessary lines and takes out any mistakes. The inker's job comes next. He inks over the remaining lines of the sketch, then hands it off to the letterer to insert the dialogue.

Ezra worked hard. At the end of the first week he found an extra fifty cents in his pay envelope, and at the end of the second week, another fifty cents. He gave most of his pay to Gussie, keeping some for brushes and paints.

In the evenings he joined his friends at Ardie's Diner, where they sat and talked for hours over five-cent cups of coffee. They had long discussions about which was best — democracy, socialism, communism, anarchy. They argued not only about politics, but about books, paintings, and the future of America.

One day, Ardie posted signs at each table: *Coffee, Ten Cents, Minimum*.

"What are you doing to us?" Ezra and his friends asked Ardie pleadingly.

"I can't make a living selling coffee for five cents — and from now on only one cup a night for each of you. I'm a poor man with a family to support."

With no place to gather, the group drifted apart. Some moved to Greenwich Village, a haven for many New York artists.

Chapter Nine

A Place of His Own

Ezra was twenty-three years old and wanted a place of his own. But how would he tell Gussie? *A fellow needs his independence,* he'd say. *A fellow needs to grow up.*

He waited until he got her alone. If Mae was there, she'd side with Gussie. If Gussie started to cry, Mae would cry, too. The women in the house always stuck together. He'd tell her after Mae left for business school.

After Gussie finished her second cup of coffee, Ezra made his move. He announced timidly, "Ma, I'm moving out."

There was an uncomfortable silence. Gussie looked him over from head to foot. He suddenly remembered the day long ago when he ran away, when he hoped Gussie would say, "Don't leave me. I love you. Please stay at home." Instead she just tied his bundle tighter. Now he was afraid she'd say, "What will become of us if you move out?" But again she surprised him, asking instead, "Who will take care of you?"

"I can take care of myself."

"Remember how sick you were when you were a little boy? How once we had to take you to the hospital? How I always had to remind you to wear a sweater, take a scarf, keep out of drafts? Even when I was sick, I took good care of you! And now — nothing! Just, 'I'm moving out'!"

Gussie stopped talking. She just stood and stared at him, shaking her head sadly.

"Ma. I'll send you money just as if I was still here."

"Money!" she repeated as if the word were an insult. "We won't need your money. In a few months Mae finishes her bookkeeping course. The teacher says she's the best student in the class. She'll get a job as a bookkeeper and earn ten dollars a week to start, like Mrs. Wolf's daughter, Sadie."

"I'll send you money anyway, and come see you every week. I'll be back for my things as soon as I find a place," Ezra said quickly and bolted for the door. It was one of the hardest things he ever had to do.

It was easy to find apartments in those days. There were lots of vacancies during the Depression. People lost their jobs, their money ran out, and they couldn't pay their rent. They got warnings from the landlord, and if they still couldn't pay, they were evicted — thrown out onto the street, furniture and all.

When Ezra was in high school he and his friends saw lots of evicted families. He and his classmates waited until the authorities left, then helped the families move back in. Sometimes they had rent parties. Friends and neighbors brought food and a few dollars, and they all had a party. The rent got paid and the families had their homes back — for another month, at least.

Ezra wanted a top floor apartment with a skylight. He heard of one and he hurried to see it. It was a fourth floor walk-up near Greenwich Village. An elevated train roared past every few minutes, rattling everything in the apartment that wasn't nailed down. Nathan, the man vacating the apartment, was an artist, too. He pointed to the skylight. "It's very good for painting," he said. "And you'll get used to the noise."

Nathan wore a pith helmet, the kind worn by African explorers. Ezra thought it was a little peculiar, but figured some artists are just a little strange.

"Why are you moving out?" asked Ezra.

"I need more space. I hate to leave, though. I did some good painting here — even sold two."

"I'm sure this will be a good place for me," Ezra said. "Let's see the rest of it. Where's the kitchen? And the bathroom?"

Nathan opened a closet door. Inside was a small sink wedged into a corner, a wooden icebox, a table with an electric hot plate on it, and a shelf with a few pots.

"There's a toilet in the hall for tenants on this floor. When I want a shower I go to the public baths on 23rd Street. It's no trouble. And just look at that skylight!"

"I'll take it!" Ezra said enthusiastically. Then, almost as an afterthought, he asked, "How much is it?"

"Eighteen dollars a month," Nathan said.

Eighteen dollars a month. Almost one week's salary at Five-Star Comics! He needed ten dollars a week for Gussie and Mae. Maybe he'd get some extra work at Five-Star. Maybe he'd get a raise.

"I'll leave you some of the furniture — the cot and the table and the kitchen stuff," Nathan offered.

"Okay, thanks." Ezra was sure this would be a great place for him.

"One more thing," Nathan said. "The bell doesn't

They got warnings from the landlord, and if they then couldn't pay, they were evicted — thrown out on the street, furniture and all. (Detail from *Regards to the Man in the Moon*, 1981.)

work. My friends call me from the street. It works out fine."

Just then, a train roared by. Ezra saw the passengers peering out at him from the windows. He was sure he'd get used to the noise.

He went home to get his things. It was late when he returned and he was tired. He lay down on the cot near the window of his new apartment and stared up at the skylight until he fell asleep.

The screech of a passing train woke him with a start. *Where am I?* he wondered. He sat up abruptly, hitting his head on the sloping ceiling. BANG!

He got up, rubbed his head, and explored the room. For the first time he noticed that the only place he could stand up straight was in the middle of the room. That's where he stood earlier that day.

He heard someone call his name from the street. He hurried to the window, bumping his head again on the ceiling. THUD! Now he knew why Nathan wore a pith helmet. He wished Nathan had left that behind, too.

In the evenings he met his friends at the Life Cafeteria on Sheridan Square. It was like Ardie's Diner, only much bigger. And some of the people there were well-known artists and writers. He was living in the most exciting city in America.

His life was filled with work, discussing current affairs with cronies at the cafeteria, and of course, painting.

But the world was changing rapidly. Civil war broke out

in Spain. And in 1939 Germany invaded Poland. World War II had begun.

When he was in high school, Ezra and his classmates believed that world peace was the answer to every problem. He belonged to the Peace Club in school and marched with banners and signs promoting peace. It was a bold step because the students who marched cut classes. But they believed fervently in world peace.

Hitler put an end to any dreams of world peace. He was an evil power that had to be stopped. Ezra heard his mother crying over the plight of the Jews in the "Old Country."

In 1943, he joined the Army. He didn't worry about Gussie and Mac. He'd send them his army pay. He wanted to go overseas, perhaps even help liberate Paris from the Nazis.

But the Army took advantage of Ezra's artistic talents instead. He was assigned to a unit in Florida where he designed camouflage patterns. Camouflage was used to disguise churches, monuments, and museums. When enemy pilots flew over these structures, they'd think they were flying over a forest. Ezra's work was important.

Two years later, the war ended. It was a glorious time for America and her allies. Hitler was defeated, and peace was restored to Europe.

Ezra was discharged from the Army in 1945 and returned home. Mae was working now. She and Gussie had moved from Brooklyn to Queens, another borough of New York City. It was a good move. Gussie didn't have to climb so many stairs, and Mae could walk to work. From their kitchen window they saw birds and trees and sidewalks lined with flowers, not garbage cans.

It was the home Gussie always wanted. And she kept it as neat as a pin. There were lace curtains on the windows, an embroidered tablecloth, a canary, a photograph of Ezra in uniform, and paintings on every wall — Ezra's paintings, as well as Gussie's and Mae's. They had started painting, too.

Gussie made dinner and they all sat comfortably, talking about Ezra's assignments in the Army and Mae's new job. When he rose to leave, Gussie asked, "Where are you going, Ezra? What are your plans now?"

"I don't know. I'll stay with a friend for a while. I'll think of something," he answered half-heartedly.

The truth was he had no plans, no job, no place to live, and no family of his own. He felt as if he was in a long, narrow corridor. The door at one end had slammed shut, closing off one part of his life. The door at the other end had not yet opened.

Tragically, hatred of Jews did not end with Hitler's defeat. In 1947, anti-Jewish sentiment was prevalent even in America. It was hard to find work if you were Jewish. "Jews need not apply," newspaper ads read. Many Jews changed their names in order to "fit in." Ezra thought it was shameful to deny one's heritage. But eventually he, too, made the painful decision to change his name. On February 8, 1948, and forever thereafter, Jack Ezra Katz was known as Ezra Jack Keats.

Chapter Ten

Paris Artist/ New York Illustrator

Ezra dreamed of seeing Paris ever since his first visit to a museum. It was the home of many artists he admired. Now that Gussie and Mae were settled, he was free to realize his dream. With a borrowed suitcase, his easel, and his paints, Ezra sailed for France. It was 1949.

He found a room in a small boarding house in Montmartre, the artists' quarter. The room was tiny; its walls covered with yellow striped wallpaper. There was a table and chair, a narrow bed, a small sink, and a window from which he could see the rooftops of Paris, rooftops dotted with tiny chimney pots.

The room cost five francs a night, including breakfast. Ezra made some quick calculations. At that rate he could stay in Paris for at least three months. He'd have money for modest evening meals, for canvas and for paint.

"*Oui*, yes, *oui*," Ezra said, nodding his head and smiling to make certain his new landlady understood his feeble French.

"One week in advance," the landlady replied. She pointed to his easel and paints and added, "Artists pay one week in advance."

It must be hard for artists to make a living in Paris, too, Ezra thought. He agreed to pay, extending a handful of French money which the old woman deftly picked over, leaving a only few coins behind. He kept his U.S. dollars in his shoe. He would convert them into French francs the next day.

Ezra unpacked his suitcase and carefully arranged his brushes and paints on the little wooden table. It was late now and he was tired from his long journey. He lay down on the narrow bed to rest, but his head was spinning. He was full of wonder and excitement over what the morning would bring. *Would this night ever end?*

With the first light of dawn, Ezra set out to explore the city. Paris was even more beautiful than he had imagined. All the images he'd kept in his head were being set to music — the music of Paris — muffled footsteps on narrow cobblestone streets, a tinkling bell in a bake shop announcing the day's first customer.

Ezra walked for hours up and down tiny winding streets — streets so narrow you could reach across and stir your neighbor's coffee, if you dared. He drew as he walked, sketching scenes he would later paint — outdoor cafes, flower stalls, the clockmaker's shop. He returned to his room very late that first night, his notebook bursting with sketches.

For the next several weeks Ezra left the boarding house early each morning with his easel and paints. One morning as he was putting the finishing touches on a painting he'd started the day before, he was distracted by a very peculiar sound. He turned to find an old woman peering over his shoulder. She pointed to his painting as she smacked her lips loudly. "*Delicieux*," she commented, "*delicieux. Je voudrais bien acheter ce tableau, monsieur. Combien*?" [Delicious, delicious. I'd like to buy this painting, mister. How much?]

Ezra couldn't believe his ears. Did she actually want to *buy* his painting? He graciously accepted the twenty francs note she offered and handed her the canvas still wet with paint. He watched her toddle off, beckoning to neighbors to come see what she'd bought.

Ezra sold several more paintings during those first few months, some at much higher prices. As a result, he extended his stay to almost a year, painting almost every day. On Sundays he visited museums and browsed through the bookstalls along the banks of the Seine River. He bought old prints, which he hung on the walls of his tiny rented room.

Soon after his arrival in Paris, Ezra bought himself a beret which he wore faithfully. Why, with easel, paint box, and beret, he looked just like a Frenchman.

One day, while he sketched one of the beautiful bridges

that link the banks of the Seine, he noticed a man watching him from across the street. After a few moments the man approached, looked at Ezra's drawing, and said in perfect English, "It's very beautiful."

Ezra thanked him and asked why he addressed him in English. "Your shoes, my good man. Your shoes. They are American, no?"

They are American, yes, Ezra thought, *and so am I. Perhaps it is time to go home and settle down.*

When he returned to New York, Ezra sold the rest of his Paris paintings. He rented a small basement apartment on Washington Avenue in Brooklyn. It had a back yard with a picnic table and benches. That summer he sat out back regaling his new neighbors with stories of his year abroad.

One evening a neighbor who knew Ezra's work very well suggested he look for work in publishing. Publishing houses are always looking for artists and illustrators, she explained.

So, every day for months Ezra made the rounds of the New York publishing houses where he left samples of his work.

"Thank you very much," came the replies. "We'll call you if we ever need your style of drawing."

His money was almost gone. He spent sleepless nights worrying about his next meal and next month's rent. *What good are his paintings? Will they fill his belly when he is hungry?* He heard his father's voice over and over in his head. Was

A Paris street scene. (Self-portrait.)

Benjamin right all along? Should he abandon his painting and find other work?

Then, just when Ezra was losing all hope, a neighbor knocked at his door. "Hey, Keats, there's a call for you."

Ezra bounded upstairs to the telephone that hung in the hallway. "Hello," he said tentatively. "Yes, this is Ezra Keats." It was a publisher — a publisher who liked his work. Ezra had his first assignment. That job led to others, and gradually he began to establish himself in publishing, creating book jackets for works by various authors.

One of the books was prominently displayed in the window of Doubleday Bookshop on Fifth Avenue. A children's book editor saw it and liked it. She asked Ezra to illustrate a book called *Jubilant for Sure*, by Elizabeth Hubbard Lansing, a nurse who traveled throughout the Smoky Mountains in Tennessee ministering to the poor.

When she asked if he knew anything about the Smoky Mountains, he replied, "No," hoping his honesty wouldn't cost him the assignment.

"No problem," came the reply. "When can you leave?"

Two days later he was on his way to Tennessee. As soon as he arrived, he set off with his sketchbook, hitching a ride into the hilly countryside on an old farm truck. There he discovered the world Elizabeth Hubbard Lansing described so skillfully in her book — gentle rolling hills dotted with tiny wooden shacks and acres and acres of tobacco crops.

Ezra saw a tiny ramshackle house at the end of a dirt road

Ezra saw a tiny ramshackle house at the end of a dirt road and signaled to the driver to let him off. (Detail from *Clementina's Cactus*, 1982.)

and signaled to the driver to let him off. The front yard was cluttered with farm tools. Pigs snorted and chickens clucked contentedly in the early morning sun. He began to sketch diligently, glancing from the scene to his sketchbook and back again. A barefoot child strolled into his line of vision. She wore a tattered smock and calico sun bonnet. She stood staring at Ezra, who was intent on his work. Without saying a word, he included her in his sketch.

"Hello there," came a voice from inside the house. "You lookin' for somethin'?"

The screen door opened and a tall, lanky man with a shotgun slung over his arm stepped out onto the porch.

"No," shouted Ezra. "I'm here to draw pictures." He held his open sketchbook high above his head. "See?" he asked.

Ezra explained that he was illustrating a children's book about the Smoky Mountains.

"How 'bout somethin' cool to drink?" asked the man, holding the screen door open and motioning Ezra inside.

"Thank you," Ezra replied. He made his way toward the house, causing a stampede of cackling hens.

Inside, he met the whole family and was invited to stay as long as he liked. Over the next several days he filled his sketchbook with wonderful drawings and swapped stories about New York City for marvelous mountain tales.

Jubilant for Sure, published in 1954, was received as one of the best illustrated books of that year. Ezra's career in children's books had begun.

Chapter Eleven

The Snowy Day

Ezra's assignments increased steadily. He illustrated covers and stories for magazines like *Colliers*, *Readers Digest*, and *Esquire* and continued to illustrate books. The projects were interesting, and he enjoyed researching them.

Over the years, he amassed a large collection of pictures clipped from newspapers and magazines. They were pictures of things that interested him, things he might use in his work. In the collection was a series of photographs of a beautiful little black boy. Ezra hung these photos on the wall of his studio, along with others he especially liked. They remained there for years, then were filed away and forgotten.

In the winter of 1961, he began work on a children's book that changed his life. One evening, he and his friends were reminiscing about their childhood days in the snow. Ezra decided to illustrate a book about it. He would write it, too.

While thumbing through his picture collection looking for snow scenes, he rediscovered the photographs of the little boy. He realized that none of the children's books he had illustrated thus far featured a black child as the hero. This little boy would be his hero. He called him Peter.

Ezra worked on his book every evening after he finished his other assignments. He had fun creating Peter's world. He used techniques he'd never used before, cutting buildings out of brightly colored paper and pasting them onto his canvas.

He found books of fabric samples in a local upholstery shop and cut out linen sheets for Peter's bed, pajamas for him to sleep in, and a snowsuit to keep him warm. He lined the walls of Peter's room with bright red fabric.

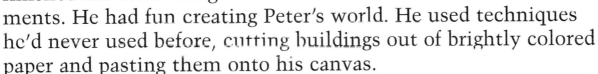

He painted mounds and mounds of pink and purple snow. To make snowflakes, he carved erasers into different patterns and shapes, dipped them in pink, blue, and green paint and stamped them on his drawing. He soaked a toothbrush with black paint and ran his thumb across its bristles to create shadows in Peter's bedroom at night. And finally, he put words to his

ABOVE: He rediscovered photographs of the little boy.
(Photo by Dr. Bert Malone, LIFE Magazine, May 13th, 1940.)
LEFT: He cut out linen sheets for Peter's bed, and pajamas for
him to sleep in. (Detail from *The Snowy Day*, 1962.)

story — the story of Peter's adventures in the snow. Ezra called his book *The Snowy Day*.

He worked steadily with an ease and freedom he had never known before. It seemed like the book was creating itself. *The Snowy Day* was published by Viking Press in 1962.

Soon after its publication, Ezra received a surprising phone call. He heard an unfamiliar voice excitedly ask, "Mr. Keats? Mr. Ezra Jack Keats? Are you sitting down?"

"Why, yes,"Ezra replied. "I am."

"Mr. Keats," the voice continued, "your book, *The Snowy Day*, has been chosen as the best children's book of the year. We are pleased to award you the Caldecott Medal."

"Well, thank you," said Ezra. "That's very nice of you. I'm glad you like the book. I'm happy for Peter." He hung up and returned to his work.

Minutes later the phone rang again. It was his publisher. "Ezra, congratulations! Do you know what this means? You've been awarded one of the highest honors in children's literature. The Caldecott Medal is given to the artist of the most distinguished American picture book. You're a success, man. They love it!"

Ezra was astonished. How strange, he thought. Why all the fuss? *The Snowy Day* was a joy to create, almost effortless. In it he had combined the things he knew best—painting, storytelling, and kids. He was good at

painting and storytelling and, after all, he'd been a kid once himself.

Ezra was forty-seven years old. Gussie and Willie had died and only Mae remained to share in his success.

"You must keep on painting," Max Weber said as he left Ezra at the train station almost thirty years earlier. "Don't let anything discourage you."

Finally it seemed, he had found a place for his art.

ABOVE: The Caldecott Medal is given to the artist of the most distinguished American picture book. (Cover of *The Snowy Day*, 1962.)

Chapter Twelve

Ezra's Legacy

Ezra continued to write and illustrate children's books until his death in 1983. *The Snowy Day*'s hero, Peter, is featured in several other books including *Peter's Chair* and *Whistle for Willie*.

Ezra was encouraged by the honors he won. But most of all, he was encouraged by letters from his readers. Sometimes they included gifts — chewing gum, postage stamps, pennies, even photographs of his young admirers. Ezra read every letter carefully and answered each one.

Some of them made him smile — like the little girl who wrote asking how Ezra stayed inside the lines when he colored the pictures in his books. Some of them made him proud — like the little boy who wanted to be an artist like Ezra when he grew up. The children often sent drawings, imitating Ezra's style. They drew pictures of their favorite Keats characters.

Schoolchildren around the country wrote to him. Sometimes they called him on the telephone and his voice was carried over the public address system so everyone could hear. One particular telephone conversation went like this:

"Hello, Mr. Keats, are you married?" a little girl asked.

"No," said Ezra, "regrettably I am not."

"Well, how many children do you have?" came the next question.

"The characters in my books are my children," Ezra replied.

It was true, thought Ezra; although he had never married and had no children of his own, he was a parent to all the characters he created in his books — Peter, of course, Archie in *Goggles!* (a Caldecott Honor book), Louie in a book by that name, Jenny, Maggie, and many more.

Ezra was often invited to visit schools to meet his fans. One particular school in Oregon invited him for a very special reason — the children planned a parade. Ezra was the guest of honor. He rode in a white convertible with the top down, while the children marched behind him dressed like characters from his books. There were mice and cats and garbage cans. Afterwards, Ezra said he'd never shaken hands with so many garbage cans!

Over the years, his books were translated into several languages, including Japanese, German, French, and Arabic. He began to get letters from children overseas.

Skates, the story of two dogs' adventures on roller

skates, was published in 1973. The book was very popular in Japan. Children there began to rollerskate all around Tokyo. Their parents petitioned the mayor to build a skating rink where they could skate safely, free of the dangers of city traffic. The rink was built and dedicated to Ezra. A plaque bearing his name shines there to this day, and rollerskating remains a popular pastime in Japan.

Ezra's work became more and more popular. UNICEF, an international organization dedicated to the welfare of children, asked him to design a series of greeting cards. The sale of these cards raised almost half a million dollars for children in Asia, Africa, and South America.

Some of his best loved books were made into films. In 1967, he was invited by the Empress of Iran to an international children's film festival that featured the film of his book, *Whistle for Willie.*

In 1971, a library in Warrensville, Ohio, named its reading room after Ezra, and a rocking chair in a Burlington, North Carolina library bears a plaque boasting "Ezra Jack Keats sat here."

The University of Southern Mississippi awarded a special medal to Ezra for his contribution to children's literature, in 1980.

Clementina's Cactus, Ezra's last book, was published in 1982. It is a storybook without words about a spirited little girl who lives with her father near the Arizona desert.

In March of 1983, Ezra began research on a book set in

Israel, a place he longed to see. He celebrated his birthday that year at the Youth Wing Library of the Israel Museum where librarians, teachers, and students gathered to hear him speak, and to see films of his books, among them *The Snowy Day* and *Apt. 3*. He was 67 years old.

As a tribute to Ezra, the Youth Wing Library offers a special Ezra Jack Keats Story Hour every Tuesday and Thursday at 4:00 in the afternoon.

When he returned to New York, Ezra was invited to participate in a very exciting project. One of his most popular books, *The Trip*, was being set to music. It is the story of a lonely little boy's imaginary plane ride back to his old neighborhood. Ezra was asked to design the costumes and scenery.

His health was failing now and he tired easily. Nevertheless, while sketching the costumes and scenery for *The Trip*, he followed his usual routine. He sat in his big, brown chair near the window of his Manhattan studio with Samantha, his cat, asleep at his side.

He spent a lot of time sitting near the window with Samantha these days. Sometimes they just looked out at the sky. Samantha was fascinated by the clouds that floated by. Ezra thought back many years ago to his first painting — the little white cloud Tzadik inspired him to paint.

How far he had come! It was a difficult journey at times, but always an exciting one. And he remembered it all vividly.

The Trip is the story of a lonely little boy's imaginary plane ride back to his old neighborhood. (Spread from *The Trip*, 1979.)

In April, 1983, he was hospitalized with severe chest pains. His colleagues brought him a recording of the music for *The Trip* which he played over and over again during his hospital stay.

Ezra died in New York Hospital on May 6, 1983. Two days later *The Trip* opened to rave reviews at the first All Children's Theater in Manhattan.

His rich, painterly illustrations and simple, touching stories revolutionized children's literature. He won international acclaim for accomplishments that exceeded his own expectations. And though his death is a tragic loss to many, Ezra Jack Keats lives on in the hearts and minds of the children who read his books and in the memory of those who love him.

Books by Ezra Jack Keats

The reader is invited to read, or read again, the books of Ezra Jack Keats.

(Ezra often included himself and his cat, Samantha, in his illustrations. Now that you've met them, see if you can find them in some of his later books.)

The Snowy Day (1962)

Whistle for Willie (1964)

Jennie's Hat (1966)

Peter's Chair (1967)

A Letter to Amy (1968)

Goggles! (1969)

Hi, Cat! (1970)

Apt. 3 (1971)

Pet Show! (1972)

Pssst! Doggie (1973)

Skates (1973)

Dreams (1974)

Kitten for a Day (1974)

Louie (1975)

The Trip (1978)

Maggie and the Pirate (1979)

Louie's Search (1980)

Regards to the Man in the Moon (1981)

Clementina's Cactus (1982)

List of Illustrations

Index